For all of the parents
and caregivers whose lives
have been touched
by the Coronavirus.

We are all in this together.

Published in 2020 by Kelley Donner
www.kelleydonner.com

First Edition 2020
ISBN 978-1-7339595-8-2

The Day the Lines Changed

Written and illustrated by

Kelley Donner

The green line was a happy line.

She lived with her mom and dad
and her sister and brother.

Her grandmother lived
with them, too.

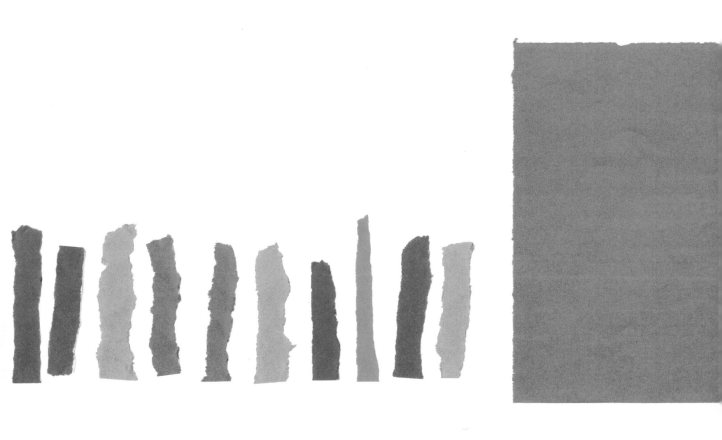

She went to school.

And on the weekends,
her family went to the town square.

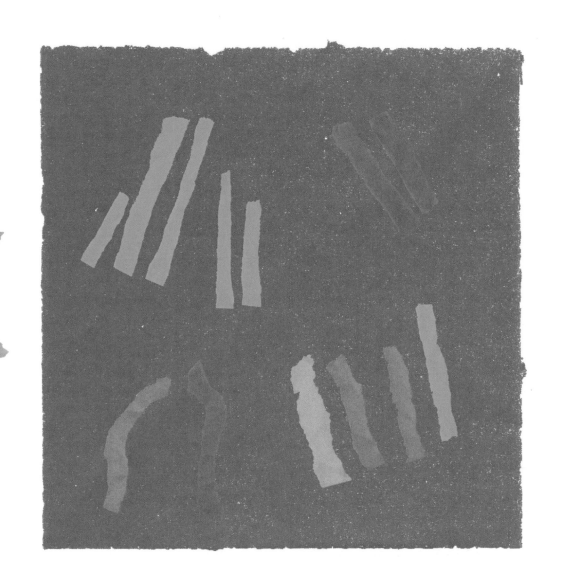

Then one day,
some of the orange
lines in town
became crooked.

And then,
it also happened
to the
purple lines.

The green family was worried they might become crooked as well.

Fortunately, most of the lines
who became crooked were able
to straighten out again.

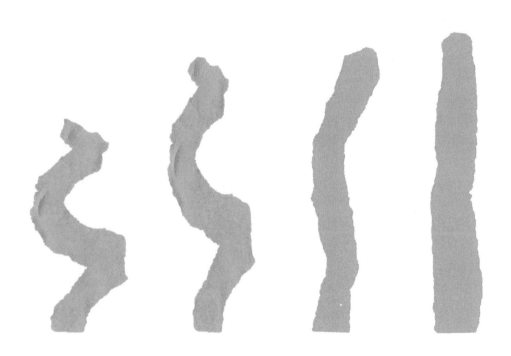

Unfortunately, many older lines
became so crooked that they fell apart.

The lines weren't sure what to do.
In order to protect the older lines
from becoming crooked, they decided
to stop meeting altogether.

The children
were no longer able
to go to school.

And, the town square was empty.

The green line was worried.
Would their lives ever
be the same again?

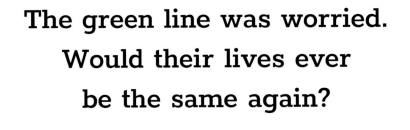

But then something
exciting happened.

One line made a spot which stopped the
lines from becoming crooked.

Soon all the lines wanted to get
a spot. The lines got in a line.

The younger lines let the older
lines go first.

The green line could go to school again.

And on the weekend,
her family went to the town square.

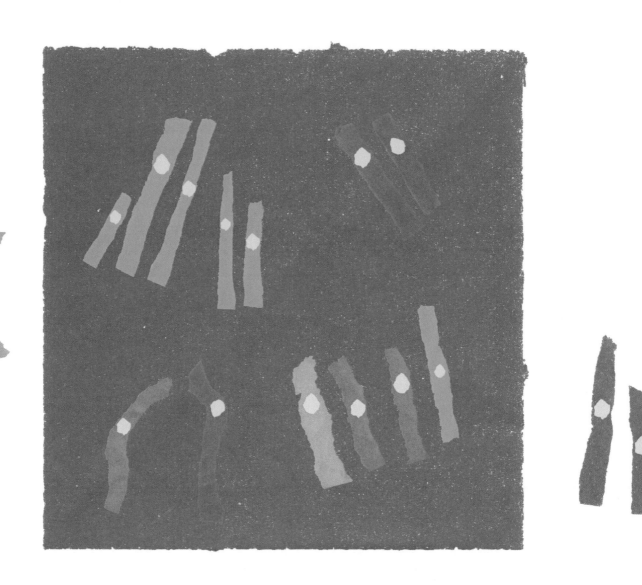

The green line was happy again.

Acknowledgements:

It was not easy trying to write, illustrate, and design this book while being quarantined with three young boys whose lives drastically changed due to the Coronavirus. Worried about their future, their grandparents, and whether or not they could play football, their questions inspired me to think about how children relate to a pandemic. Without their inspiration, I would never have been able to write this story, let alone come up with the idea.

Therefore, a great thank you goes out to my entire family for your love, support, and patience.